Bobcat
or
Lynx?

by Mari Schuh

BLASTOFF! READERS

BELLWETHER MEDIA · MINNEAPOLIS, MN

Blastoff! Readers are carefully developed by literacy experts to build reading stamina and move students toward fluency by combining standards-based content with developmentally appropriate text.

Level 1 provides the most support through repetition of high-frequency words, light text, predictable sentence patterns, and strong visual support.

Level 2 offers early readers a bit more challenge through varied sentences, increased text load, and text-supportive special features.

Level 3 advances early-fluent readers toward fluency through increased text load, less reliance on photos, advancing concepts, longer sentences, and more complex special features.

★ **Blastoff! Universe**

LEVELS

Reading Level

Grade
K

Grades
1–3

Grade
4

This edition first published in 2022 by Bellwether Media, Inc.

No part of this publication may be reproduced in whole or in part without written permission of the publisher. For information regarding permission, write to Bellwether Media, Inc., Attention: Permissions Department, 6012 Blue Circle Drive, Minnetonka, MN 55343.

Library of Congress Cataloging-in-Publication Data

LC record for Bobcat or Lynx? available at https://lccn.loc.gov/2021039718

Editor: Elizabeth Neuenfeldt   Designer: Laura Sowers

Printed in the United States of America, North Mankato, MN.

Table of Contents

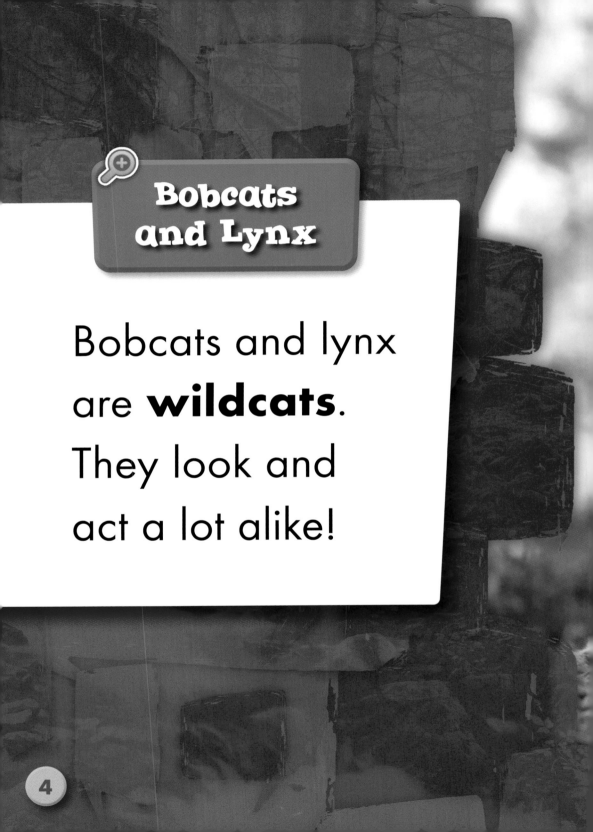

Bobcats and lynx are **wildcats**. They look and act a lot alike!

lynx

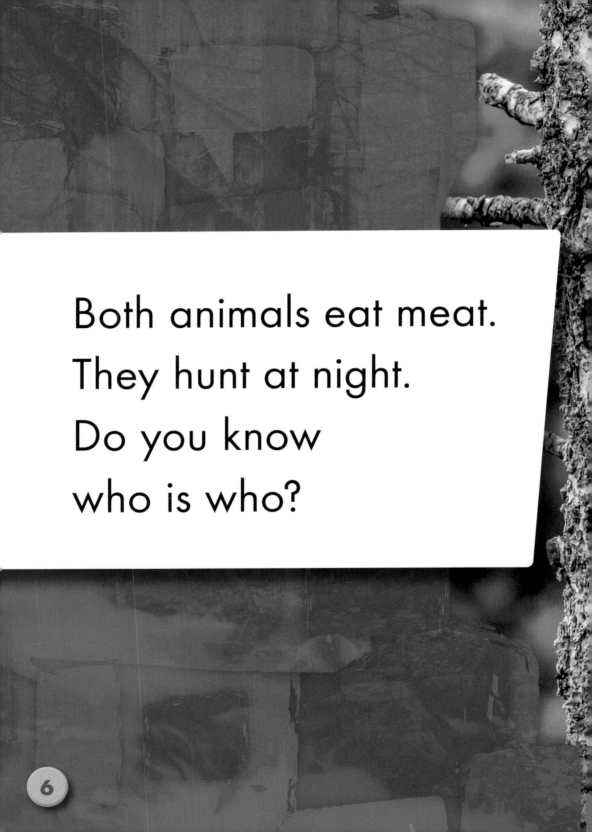

Both animals eat meat.
They hunt at night.
Do you know
who is who?

bobcat

Different Looks

Lynx have
long ear **tufts**.
Bobcat ear tufts
are shorter.

tufts

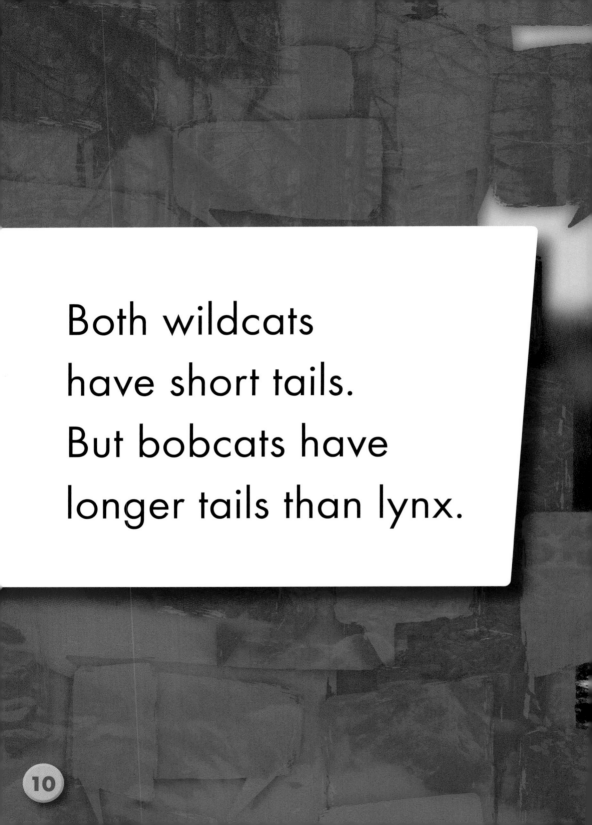

Both wildcats
have short tails.
But bobcats have
longer tails than lynx.

Big, furry paws help lynx walk on snow. Bobcat paws are **bare** on the bottom.

bare
paw

Lynx have longer legs than bobcats. This helps lynx hunt in deep snow.

Both wildcats can jump. But lynx can jump farther than bobcats.

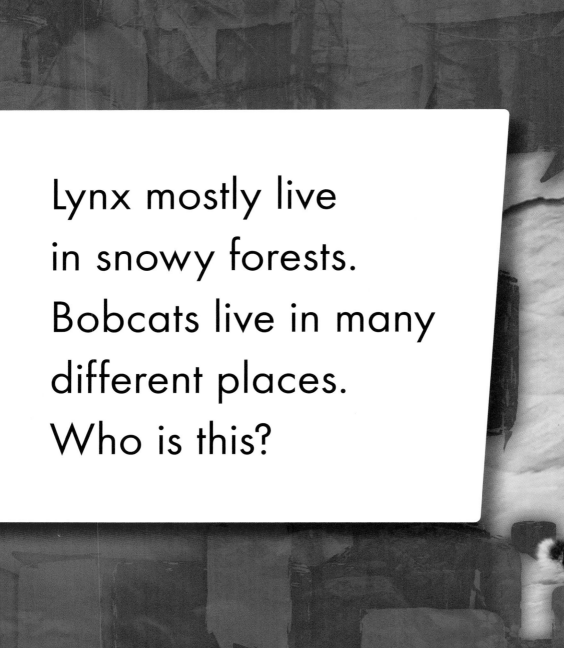

Lynx mostly live
in snowy forests.
Bobcats live in many
different places.
Who is this?

shorter ear tufts

longer tail

shorter legs

bottom of paws are bare

Bobcat Differences

cannot jump as far as lynx

live in many different places

longer ear tufts

shorter
tail

longer legs

big, furry paws

Lynx Differences

jump farther
than bobcats

live in snowy
forests

21

Glossary

bare

not covered

wildcats

kinds of cats that live in the wild

tufts

small bunches of fur on top of an animal's ears

To Learn More

AT THE LIBRARY

Carney, Elizabeth. *Wild Cats*. Washington, D.C.: National Geographic, 2017.

Perish, Patrick. *Lynx*. Minneapolis, Minn.: Bellwether Media, 2022.

Thielges, Alissa. *Bobcats*. Mankato, Minn.: Amicus Ink, 2021.

ON THE WEB

FACTSURFER

Factsurfer.com gives you a safe, fun way to find more information.

1. Go to www.factsurfer.com.

2. Enter "bobcat or lynx" into the search box and click 🔍.

3. Select your book cover to see a list of related content.

Index

The images in this book are reproduced through the courtesy of: moosehenderson, cover (bobcat); Agnieszka Bacal, cover (lynx); Karel Bartik, pp. 4-5; Janet Horton/ Alamy, pp. 6-7; Carolina K. Smith MD, pp. 8-9; slowmotiongli, p. 9 (bobcat); lorenz, pp. 10-11; miroslav chytil, p. 11 (lynx); Danita Delimont, pp. 12-13, 20 (jump); Jack Nevitt, p. 13 (bobcat); Jukka Jantunen, pp. 14-15; Don Mammoser, pp. 15 (bobcat), 18-19, 20 (live), 22 (wildcats); Sarah Cheriton-Jones, pp. 16-17; Warren Metcalf, p. 20 (bobcat); Erni, p. 21 (lynx); Grindstone Media Group, p. 21 (jump); Ghost Bear, p. 21 (live); Diane079F, p. 22 (bare); Matt Knoth, p. 22 (hunt); Kev Gregory, p. 22 (tufts).